T0266008

THE MINING ROAD

Leanne O'Sullivan was born in 1983, and comes from the Beara peninsula in West Cork. She received an MA in English in 2006 from University College, Cork, where she now teaches. The winner of several of Ireland's poetry competitions in her early 20s (including the Seacat, Davoren Hanna and RTE Rattlebag Poetry Slam), she has published four collections, all from Bloodaxe: *Waiting for My Clothes* (2004); *Cailleach: The Hag of Beara* (2009), winner of the Rooney Prize for Irish Literature in 2010; *The Mining Road* (2013); and *A Quarter of an Hour* (2018), winner of the inaugural Farmgate Café National Poetry Award 2019. *A Quarter of an Hour* was also shortlisted for the *Irish Times* Poetry Now Award 2019 and the Pigott Poetry Prize 2019.

She was given the Ireland Chair of Poetry Bursary Award in 2009 and the Lawrence O'Shaughnessy Award for Irish Poetry in 2011, and received a UCC Alumni Award in 2012.

Leanne O'Sullivan

THE MINING ROAD

BLOODAXE BOOKS

Copyright © Leanne O'Sullivan 2013

ISBN: 978 1 85224 968 7

First published 2013 by
Bloodaxe Books Ltd,
Eastburn,
South Park,
Hexham,
Northumberland NE46 1BS.

www.bloodaxebooks.com
For further information about Bloodaxe titles
please visit our website and join our mailing list
or write to the above address for a catalogue.

Supported by
**ARTS COUNCIL
ENGLAND**

LEGAL NOTICE

All rights reserved. No part of this book may be
reproduced, stored in a retrieval system, or
transmitted in any form, or by any means, electronic,
mechanical, photocopying, recording or otherwise,
without prior written permission from Bloodaxe Books Ltd.

Requests to publish work from this book
must be sent to Bloodaxe Books Ltd.

Leanne O'Sullivan has asserted her right under
Section 77 of the Copyright, Designs and Patents Act 1988
to be identified as the author of this work.

Cover design: Neil Astley & Pamela Robertson-Pearce.

This is a digital reprint of the 2013 Bloodaxe Books edition.

for my Grandmothers
Brigie Sullivan,
Rita O'Sullivan

ACKNOWLEDGEMENTS

Acknowledgements are due to the editors of the following publications in which some of these poems first appeared: *Cliché: Poems for Cork Simon at 40*, *The Clifden Anthology*, *The Irish Times*, *The Moth*, *New Hibernia Review*, *The Oxford Magazine*, *Peut-être: revue poétique et philosophique*, *Poetry London*, *Ropes*, *The SHOp*, *Southword*, *Sunday Miscellany* (broadcast on RTE Radio 1), *The Stinging Fly*, www.connotationpress.com and www.poetryinternational.org.

Thank you to the Arts Council of Ireland/An Chomhairle Ealaíon for a generous bursary in 2010, which helped me to complete this collection.

I am very grateful to Mr Connie Murphy, Beara teacher and historian, for his generosity in providing me with material about the mines and for the inspiring conversations, and to Emma McCarthy for her help with my translating and re-creating the description of 'Fraoch'.

My thanks are also due to Pat Cotter and Jennifer Matthews at the Munster Literature Centre; the Center for Irish Studies, University of St Thomas, St Paul, Minnesota for the Lawrence O'Shaughnessy Award for Irish Poetry, 2011; to the United States Ambassador and Mrs Rooney for the Rooney Prize for Irish Literature, 2010; to Michael Longley for nominating me for the Ireland Chair of Poetry Bursary Award 2009; to the Shanghai Writers Association for a residency in 2009; to Le Centre Culturel Irlandais for a residency in 2010; and to the staff at the Tyrone Guthrie Centre, Annaghmakerrig, where some of these poems were written.

The title of the poem, 'You Were Born at Mealtime' is a phrase taken from the novel *Tarry Flynn* by Patrick Kavanagh. The phrase 'toe the ash' is borrowed from Dermot Healy's memoir *The Bend for Home*.

I would also like to thank my husband, Andrew, for his care and support while I was writing these poems.

Finally, love and thanks to my parents, Maureen and Donal, for giving me the room to write this collection and for all their support.

CONTENTS

THE ROAD

13 Townland

14 You Were Born at Mealtime

15 Irish Weather

16 Parcel

18 The Mining Road

19 Oracle

20 House Lore

22 Love Stories

23 Lightening

24 Antique Cabinets

25 Vincit Qui Se Vincit

26 Song

27 Cuckoo-spirit

28 Argos

29 Brigie

30 The Boundary Journey

32 The Lights of New York

34 Endeavour

THE STORE

37 Storehouse

38 Man Engine

43 Safe House

45 Puxley Castle, Dunboy

46 Heirloom

47 Hearing Mass

48 Polaris

49 Neighbour

51 Fraoch

52 Valentine

53 Departures

54 Car Phone

55   Sparrow

56   Station Mass

57   The Glimmerman

58   A Healing

59   Dream

61   NOTES

THE ROAD

Townland

A hankering in the skull, uttered and worked,
the stagger of heather beds cleaved in the throat;
Gorth and *Ahabrock*, and in the old stone walls
the swallows going like windborne rumours.
An ordinary night my father walking there
thought he'd heard the ghost of Norah Seer,
the border streams swelling to the sound
of her steel crutch tapping out the hours.

Old homes and a half remembered word of mouth;
we'd prowl the lanes ourselves calling her out,
the underground all moan and winnow
with disappearing streams and passages
that swept the yellowing furze. Unlistened for,
the roofless village a thousand times passed,
and beyond, the waning lift and turn of a gate,
the fall of banked moss, and all of us listening.

You Were Born at Mealtime

The empty kitchen hummed when I came home
like a swollen river with the swelling gone.
The place was all muscle in her absence,

the table laid with wintering light,
breathed and talked over day and night
for weeks. So it would all be ready.

And how often I heard our names called out
with both eyes closed – by word of mouth
my mother's children's names brought in;

a silence quickens me,
throws open the door again.

Irish Weather

(for Laura)

Rainwater gathered from the kitchen ceiling,
the blown char and armour from saucepans
spattering against the tall rim of that world.
Oh yes, that could be us two, striking
close to the sound of each word-blow;
downpour of shouts into the downstairs room,
where later we'd be kneeling at the window,
our breath stopped like white, summer pools
on the glass as we counted out minutes
between showers. The mirror of ourselves
gleaming first, we watched the sky crack open
above nests and thunder in the gutter eaves.

But lightning –

do you remember that summer in Italy?
If we moved we might have gone up in flames,
bougainvillea wavering in the valley
like us two reddened onto our chairs, the toss
of your fan being the first real crackle of fire
in the air. So that when the rain did come
and people began to hurry past us into bars
and restaurants, we sat under the dome
of the quickening sky, the stoop of the wind
lifting tables, the whole world creaked
and changed. Like once before I heard
your first shoe fall, quiet your dazzled skin.

A Parcel

Sometimes after the scatter of envelopes
he would haul a parcel from the post-van
and carry it inside for my mother

while we stood by, guessing at its greased
and sooty underside, our gazes hurried
and raised to where he left it on the table.

It smelled of heat and a stretch-marked pull
where the brown paper had worn out
against the cardboard, its sides broadening

as we picked and ferreted, sounding out
the markered names and kept distances
until the taped down edges began to give.

*

Oakside, Seventy-seven, Long Island.
The stamps my mother cut were saved
in a jam-jar while we emptied out the box,

setting the clothes in piles along the floor,
full of chatter and babbling to ourselves
as we began the slow pageant

back and forth in new shirts and dresses.
Everything being admired and considered
was hung across the curtain rail

until it seemed like a small procession
had returned home and gathered there,
breathing staleness and open air.

*

Undulant, ocean blue,
turquoise hemmed with cerise,
and a round yoke neat

and pluming at the neck.
A smock dress that swung out
below my knees

swished and swept
on its first outing around the fields.
I imagined the shiver

of an engine still beating in the hem,
traffic passing through the grasses,
thunder in the clouds.

The Mining Road

Where moss is gold in the copper pools
my mother dreams her mother on the road,
sitting up ahead, among whistled reeds

and ocean steaming rocks. Up and out
of her hospital bed, her wound stitched
and silvering beneath her night-clothes.

Quietly, she slips her cardigan off and starts
to unravel it, both hands working and steady
until she has teased it apart completely.

And begins again. Famine road, mine road,
moss stitch; like grass swallowed down a shaft
the wool quivers up again towards her lap,

her eyes cast down, needles tapping out the work,
its strangeness, until it heals her, the old
movements long clenched and deep in her hands.

I dream them now together in mountain light
leading each other where the road winds down,
and carries on, past where they thought it would end.

Oracle

...while reading, his eyes glanced over the pages...
but his voice and tongue were silent.

St Augustine's description of St Ambrose reading

I could have dozed on her sofa for hours
listening to the gathering and breaking
of the deep Atlantic edge beneath us,
the wind outside all haul and undertow
and everything around us rising.

I would have kept drifting there beside her
in the front room, but woke to the sound
of her reading to herself aloud,
her eyes weighted over the newspaper,
low and silted, ruminant mouthings,

and for a moment felt like a man stopping
quiet in a doorway to hear it,
ear to a groundswell that grew more long-ago
the longer I watched her, strange and distant
like a sudden call heard far underground.

House Lore

(after Michael Longley)

Coins Under the New House

Before you lay any other stone
unpocket any silver coins you find
and bury them in the cornerstones,

a shimmer in that darkening hollow,
good enough to trade for money-luck,
light at the door, change on the tongue.

A Cure

Wanting to find a cure make this journey
to the boundary waters between two counties,
and once you put your foot outside the door

do not speak to man nor priest nor pope
only persist on your path to the high tide mark,
pray, pray, pray and fill your bottle for home.

A House Across an Old Path

When we built on the hillside
on an old right-of-way and I cried
on the bed through the night –

                              you remember –

the long parade of voices down
past the door and that path
all untrodden in the light.

The Glowing Sod

For luck, light a sod of turf
outside the new house and follow
the fire of the evening sun,

hillside smoking your hands and face,
so the nectar of heather and earth
are the first guests at your door.

Love Stories

And when they fought, my father said,
in those day-lit, lamp-lit rooms, him bowed
into the ceremonies of the newspapers,
the sound would be of her slamming
closed the cupboard doors, the front door,
cups and plates smashed into the deep sink
like a sudden downpour of hailstones.
He would turn the pages very slowly,
so as not to disturb her, mindful of knives
where buttery spuds still plumed on the blade.

And once peering over the rim of the page
he calmly offered, 'Would you prefer a hammer?'
so that the whole thing started up again.
For three days and nights hinges turned over
the world, soft mortar crumbled somewhere
down behind the dresser, and from the eaves
the nesting starlings darted and sprung in fright,
and raised the weathered roof like a sparking flare.

Lightening

The hiss of dampness in the candle-grease,
the heavy warmth of her swaying walk
filling the room with enough light to walk by,
where the smell is of milk drying on stone

and smoke drawn out by the opening door.
She sat always in that chair, by night,
the mountain of her hands unfolding in her lap,
deep-rooted lightning halted in the sky.

Even then the only sound was her voice
bridling itself to the sea. Still I follow it,
and repeat her name in the dark, its loves
and language becoming a wading ground.

'Sit down there beside me til I tell ye all;
I saw once upon a time two swans
swimming in the bay at Ballylickey,
and himself telling me I was so beautiful.'

Antique Cabinets

So this is what I will marry into –
night drives to dig out cast-offs from a skip,
the long sweated haul, as if we had coaxed
and pulled a sleep-walked body back home
and set it up again in our own rooms.

Or another you saw at the back of a shop
found its own purchase and worked on you.
You said the shine off it was like looking
down through water, down past old wood,
a poplar sky or walnut's burred flower.

And what would I make of such an inheritance?
When you are gone and I am left wondering
what should keep of love and trees and shadows,
I imagine myself not surprised to find
the settled world steady among your things.

Vincit Qui Se Vincit

(for Joy)

On the phone from Toronto you tell us
April has arrived with her settled airs.
This morning in your garden snow lies
in wilting pools over the grasses and beds
and you think of all the hidden flowers
they told you would never grow there –

Verbena, Sweet William, Canterbury Bells
unpeeling in the dew-clear summer –
and remember too those bright ones cut
and arranged for the high assembly halls
of your wartime English boarding school,
whose motto you misheard among the rifts.

Winky, Kissy, Winky, you thought it went.
And what's this coming through just now,
in a whiteness where the eye mislays itself?
Something seen clearly when seen askew
like a boat glimpsed lightly on the mist, or
your snowdrops kindling against the snow.

Song

As if through a gap in the floorboards
of a dream I would make out her footfall
hourly on the stairs, and afterwards
a stillness on the landing, her breath small
and hungry for my own small breathing.
Outside, moonlight glimmered on the grasses,
the morning air was tricked with birdsong
and all through the worst of that sickness
I learned her approach towards my door,
her step gathering weight along the hallway
as each return came louder and more eager
against the steep and swollen darkening,
the way a bright chorus singing the day in
would carry on, singing it out again.

Cuckoo-spit

All through early June the spittle fattened
on the briars, hung against the green stems
like young shoots crouching, breathing out.
Then someone called it 'cuckoo-spit'
and I stooped closer as they pecked at it,
rush-tip and fingernail into the clotted sap,

dragging out the fuss and stick of bubbles
that welded in the heat, the slimy grit
holding fast to each unbending stalk,
and suddenly broke through to the small
green hopper, eyes like two pinholes
braced to the shade and unblinking.

The air was high and quick with birdsong
when I came home babbling about a mother
who'd let drop her babies from the sky –
Spittle-bird – then fly home to cuckoo
her song among a stride of fir trees,
refusing no defence against her wrongs.

Argos

All morning she waited near the cattle shed,
leapt at swallows that dived from the beams,
at flies gathering over the dung heaps.

And for this particular loss I remember Argos
who waited longer than a lifetime for his master,
keeping time by snowstorms and silage making,

the newer machines following on the last ones –
so, when my father's tractor finally turned up
the road she knew it, could hear the old splutter

and rattle making sense above all the rest,
deep in her breast, and ran out into the traffic to
throw down her body in front of him, in happiness.

Brigie

When you smile in your sleep
I think of the seal's tail
whispering above the waves,
slipping back again into the deep.

The Boundary Journey

I

Not to the boundary waters
       that part our two counties

but to the great Atlantic itself,

where pebbles rush like beads
           against your hands

and carry out cures for the dead.

Where the roar of light and tide
litters about my eyes

so I begin to see you
       and not see you

too late.

The stars that are not yet there
          glimmer like fires

beneath the breathless air.

Remember
      when we were really there once
at the unbarred pier

and the air and the light
        and the day all passed

into a break on the ocean,

and the singing
        of your hands beside me

was every permanent thing.

II

And who was it travelling with you that day
before your farther journey across to England,
showing the way, June sun warm on your back?
I believe it when you say it was just yourself,
one suitcase strapped to the back of the bike

and knowing the way all right, to bed down
for a night in Mrs Morley's guesthouse
in Castletownbere; where you stood alone
in the darkening room and levered electric light
for the first time from a switch on the wall.

The Lights of New York

His funeral was six years ago.
We wore black coats and gloves

and stood at the lip of his grave,
waiting for him to disappear.

The night before, I heard that
when he was a boy he used to sit

on the *cnocán* near his house
and imagine the lights of New York

fluttering like candles
on the miles deep horizon.

I walked out of his home
towards the same patch of grass

where he would sit and cross
his perfect limbs in meditation.

I squinted to see his face.
The horizon burned into the night,

as if the roof of the earth
had collapsed, and I dreamed

his body leaning forward, like a hunter
mapping his path in the dark.

When I touched him last his skin
was soft, like a spirit felt through flesh.

I reached out my hand. He sat calm
and quiet, carpentering his city of lights.

I heard the slow preparations
in the house, life lifting from the village,

the wind lining the sky
with unutterable thoughts.

Gently, I pressed my hands into the earth.
Dark against the pale crop, in the shadow

of a mountain, the eve of his burial,
at twilight, there I saw him.

Endeavour

15 July 2009, 11.21pm

Light from the kitchen
and then not even that
as we stirred a right-of-way
through the yard,

looking up always
for fear we'd miss it,
or what we imagined
would appear there –

the night sky mazed
and split with starburst,
misting tracks,
a climbing blast

that all of a sudden
might fall at our feet,
like a flare sent up from
the unhurt night-watch.

THE STORE

Storehouse

Where two pillars remember a way in
we will have to imagine it again,

dream the rusting bolt and door,
the evening stars breaking in the ore;

to hear the work beneath the ground
and mine the lower, darker sounds –

the heaving and hush, load by load,
and the bellowing roar of the wagon road.

Man Engine

Trial

The blast
travels upwards,
inwards
and out of sight.

Cnoc Rua –
the old route
re-shapes itself
at your feet,

welds into
the crooked stair
of the shaft.
The engine roar

that ferries
you down
shudders and gives
like any landing place,

any last held
breath
your lungs
have drawn.

Breathe,
breathe
into the heart
of it again –

Candlelight

– into the cankerhole,
the glandular dark.
Down
and down

between the burst
and deafening black.
I am always
looking back.

My own shape
in the foul air
marks the spot
where I stopped

to shield my eyes,
all the light
repealed
by clouds

of dust and ash –
but here I almost see,
can just make out
by candlelight,

at the end of the level,
a softer gold
and yellow glimmer
in the white quartz lode.

Tommyknockers

Small rappings
in the lode,
dark fluttering
across the beams.

It could be
a shiver in the earth
or a warning call
raised,

their knuckles
panic white,
timbers rasping
in their hold.

Or a tap
on my shoulder
pelting
to a stream.

Listen the glut,
the first scree
howling down
the shaft.

Listen
the mouths
that lie foul
in the water.

Sea Level

We always knew
they were mining
below the sea,
under the great bellies

of the earth –
could hear sometimes
far out
beyond the pier

the inconsolable
hammering
of those workers
ossifying in the tides,

the fill
of their shovels
streaming above them
in candlelight

towards crescent moon
or starfish,
where I wade
in the grey water,

the drag of my feet
hauling clouds
of shingle and ore
along their dressing floors.

Ascent

Perhaps this is why
I keep returning –
the dark
always ascending

and the light
retreating softly
beyond the shaft.
At nightfall

the engine hauls
you back
in ones and twos,
up past

the darkened galleries,
the sunk
knowledge
and wet quartz

blasted
and glittering among
the constellations –
starlight,

your own name
called out,
your hands entering
the world again.

Safe House

When they were beginning to build a country
some of the men came to hide in a house
where there was a family, and a child upstairs,
listening. They told him what to say if anyone

ever asked. Say they were never there.
Say there was only a family in that house.
And during the night the boy went to the room
where their bags and belongings were hidden.

He felt along the canvases, the mouldy wet
and sag of the straps. His fingers touched on
papers and coins, and lifted out the revolver,
its coolness and the weight of it in his hands.

Then he felt nothing. His blood crept slowly
and dark along the floorboards, underneath them,
and the room shook, and stood still,
and seemed to hang for a moment in that night.

When they found him they cleaned him,
his face, gently and quickly, and his mother
wrapped him in a blanket and took him
out to a corner of the farm and buried him.

Back in the house they gathered his things,
and built up a fire again in the kitchen,
burning his clothes, his shoes, all the signs
and small, clumsy turnings of a child.

And afterwards, in the freezing dark, the father
went out to find the doctor and the parish priest
to tell them what had happened, and what they
should say if anyone ever asked.

Tell them there was never a child.
Say they were never there.
There was never a home
or the found, easy measures of a family.

There was never a map that could lead back to
or out of that place, foreknown or imagined,
where the furze, the dark-rooted vetch, turned
over and over with the old ground and disappeared.

Puxley Castle, Dunboy

...being forever in the pre-trembling of a house that falls.

GALWAY KINNELL

Only toe the ash now,
remembering how they've cleared it,
raised it,
roofed away the vaulting birds
and winter's cobbled underthings,

glassed up the eyeholes and the brow –
just toe the ash now.
A sea swims again
in her grey face
and melts the quarrel of the fire.

I'll mind an old familiar sky
and starlings banking in the eaves;
words I'll keep like *dungeon, turret* –
What city in the trees?
Whose barbed chiming weeds?

And these old purses
hatching through the dawn?
I'll mind an uncle who comes striding
from the fires. Oh boys, says he,
We're all a sea door down.

Heirloom

A penny dropped
a hundred years ago
turns up beneath
our sweetheart cabbage,

but Love, we are still
out for spring roots,
honeyed wets
and their vanished tracks.

Hearing Mass

Even when the last monks had gone
the islanders on Dursey still gathered
at the cliff's mouth facing the Skellig
to hear Mass being said, and prayers
carried in over the Atlantic dark.

They stooped beneath the bare weather,
the vowelled gusts and gull cries
and strained their ears against the tide.
And now I see them in the oratory
standing with their faces bowed,

eyes closed and elbow to elbow,
the ocean sweating through their brows.
Then back again on Dursey where I
sense the cloudburst of an old desire
and come to crouch among those ghosts,

reciting above the downpour
the mouthing hum and drone of memory.
But the Skellig has passed into fog.
The wind thrums like wing-beats
all around and I cannot hear beyond it.

Polaris

If aliens visit us, the outcome would be much as when Columbus landed
in America, which didn't turn out well for the Native Americans.

STEPHEN HAWKING

The soft-shelled atmosphere is shrugging us off,
but what will happen, they say, when a reply
comes wheeling across the bottomless dark
and another life tremors against the airwaves?

I imagine it, aurora light tilting the night sky,
the constellations of all our boundary lines,
and in that moment a seal fastening over the earth
like the shut and sudden flicker of a periwinkle eye.

Neighbour

Steady as moles
her eyes drag nightly
across the road

into the lit houses,
one from one direction,
one from another

until her nose
is like a dark fruit
pressed against the glass

and her ears flick the air.
All evening
the bloodied liquors,

the fornications
suck at her breath,
knife against knife.

In the morning her voice
in the slight air rolls
them over her gate,

measured by her small hands
and fingers
that show us all the ways.

She knows me so well now;
I would happily feed
her the sweet mouthfuls

here in my bright kitchen,
and bury her there.
My smile would

crack across the glass.
I would know she was honest,
the night clear

and star-lit,
and the diaphanous nets
of her window gathering

its reflections –
barking dogs, a glitter of faces,
and the mist of her breath

washing over them,
stuffing her mouth
with its own whiteness.

Fraoch

Dotháet do thuidecht assind usci íarum...

Then Fraoch made to come out of the water –
Don't come, said Ailill, until you bring a spray
of that rowan from across the river,
beautiful and ripe its berries look to me.
So Fraoch went and broke a branch from the tree
and carried it back with him across the water.

Afterwards, Findabair remembered it, saying
that she had never seen anything so lovely,
nothing so beautiful as Fraoch moving
over the dark river, his body so lively
and light, his hair bright and fine-looking,
his eyes shifting from blue to green like weeds

stirring softly beneath the dark – so delicate,
she said, My love without a burden or blemish,
straight as a reed, carrying between his throat
and white face the red berries of the rowan bush.

Valentine

Darling, sometimes I know what love
is for when we lie together undressed
and I hold myself still across your body,
fevered waters rising from your skin

as if any second you will overflow,
flood to the cascade edge of the world.
I hold you down, clamp of salt and bone,
undoing the knotted wrack of your limbs.

You lie wide-eyed, jaw hanging open
as I drink you slowly with kisses.
When the morning rises up from beneath us,
you hear the street clatter, far away and calm.

My love I promise forever flowers will decorate
your breakfast table, colour will flow
from your rooms, and when your friends
begin those market-place rumours remember

how at night you bring your face to mine,
and run your fingers through my wild, red hair.
Remember I am your wife and all the tremulous
waters that run from your mouth are mine.

Departures

Your skin turns blue in the river mists,
when the sky is blue, but this is the liquid
come-and-go tracery of you beyond the corridor.

You stand there like the ghost of yourself
telling me things with your hands.
O love, your voice trembles softly down the glass

and refuses to be still, like evenings when the river
rose in a hush of deep clearing, I followed
the patterns of your skin as they were swept away.

Car Phone

(i.m. Ted Seer)

The dark smell of leather and metal heat
from the gleaming, half-opened door,
where we'd be hiding and pressing buttons
in our uncle's car. I imagined him driving
it across the Irish sea, or fairies pushing it
along over seaweed in the summer night,
surfacing over whirlpools and strange fish,
the roof glittering like a mink's smooth back.

Down the voiceless line shells and gravel
being swept along, shuddering in the cord
as we'd practise his slight London twang –
quick flints of vowel and common ground
when he'd approach from the small kitchen,
and when he left, gravel, static, quiet, the sea.

Sparrow

That one who came tapping at the window,
brown-suited, upright at dawn, my father
said was his father flown home for summer
to help outside where our help wouldn't do,
and began to wink and talk to the old man
about changes here, the new cow house,
or how he broke those lower fields into one,
keeping always straight and almost serious.

That was remembered again today, stirred
in the spring-ground of the milking shed
where light softens beyond the stalls
and shafts, and I heard a song thrush call,
bright, unexpected and familiar.
Where I turned, and almost began to answer.

The Station Mass

(for Rita Seer)

Everything scrubbed down and scrubbed again.
Every room followed its own lighted passage,
singing out its corners and the polished dark.
The makeshift altar set, she moved from room
to room, pelting the floors with her slippered walk.

Down in the kitchen the beautiful spread of meals,
the little locks and curls of butter flaring sunlight.
We were like her sentry guards in doorways,
barefoot, sweeping for motes and blemishes
or eyeing hiding places that suddenly stood clear.

Roses, silver, lace; the glasses breathed against.
Then the gravel-call of priest and neighbours
up the lane and we were all come and go again,
herself gone ahead of us down the last swept path,
snapping incantations, scattering light.

The Glimmerman

Let the light burn down,
Love, the night falls now.
He's not on the road,
not yet in the town.
Come away from the door,
let the light burn down.

Or sit by the window
where the lamplight shone,
all of your beauty a-glimmer,
all of the darkness gone.
Let the light burn down, Love,
let the light burn down.

And there must be light enough
for I can just make do –
the sweeping of your footfall,
the softness of your mouth.
Let the light burn down, Love,
let the light burn out.

A Healing

That first day of springtime thaw when the ice
began to melt and pour down the mountains,
I walked to the top of the old mining road
to hear all the slow loosening and letting go;
the kick-back of copper and clay from my heels,
the steady blasts following like the sound
of another person's footfall on the shale,
spirited behind me; the streams that thundered
down to disappear again underground
so the whole place was all tremble and go,
lightening into a stiller and clearer air.
I loved the copper-lit, the downhill skid and slack,
the water roaring out of time, turning back
with so much sound and rush that it seemed
to be gathering strength from ore and dust and clay,
under the shade of that green and beaten ground.

Dream

I think I could go home now
      and begin again,
turn in through the gate
      of the field where the light
dies last, lies down
      in the whispery borders.

NOTES

Vincit Qui Se Vincit: She conquers who conquers herself.

Endeavour: The spaceshuttle *Endeavour* was visible over Ireland eight minutes after its take-off in America.

Man Engine: A man engine was a mechanical contraption with moving platforms that facilitated the placement of miners into the mines.

Safe House: In the Irish War for Independence safe houses were used to shelter men hiding from the British soldiers.

Station Mass: Station Masses are traditionally held in the family homes of rural Ireland.

www.ingramcontent.com/pod-product-compliance
Lightning Source LLC
Jackson TN
JSHW080855211224
75817JS00002B/62